rihanna

ANNUAL 2012
POSY EDWARDS

MEET PRINCESS RIRI!

That incredible voice and brimming talent coupled with the tough-talking, super-sassy attitude, not to mention the gorgeous looks and killer curves that have made her an international megastar...it's a lethal combination!

But it's impossible to summon up anything other than total adoration for RiRi. An ordinary 23-year-old girl who has achieved extraordinary things, surviving a difficult childhood and heartbreak as an adult, to become one of the most phenomenally successful female stars on the planet.

WHO'S THAT CHICK?!

Wow! So you've heard her songs in the charts and you've seen her photo in magazines. But who is this chick from the tiny Caribbean island who is taking over the world? Read on to find out!

'GROWING UP, I ALWAYS SANG. BUT NO ONE EVER WAS REALLY PUSHING ME TO DO IT. IT WAS SOMETHING THAT I WANTED TO DO. SO I DEVELOPED A PERSONAL PASSION FOR IT, FELL IN LOVE WITH MUSIC AND DEVELOPED MY OWN TASTE AND STYLE.' R

FULL NAME
Robyn Rihanna Fenty

DATE OF BIRTH
20 February 1988

NATIONALITY
Bajan/Guyanese

BORN AND RAISED
Barbados (Parish of St. Michael)

HEIGHT
5'8"

EDUCATION
Combermere High School, Barbados

FAMILY
Mum Monica, Dad Ronald, little brothers Rajad and Rorey

FAVOURITE COLOURS
Anything bright!

FAVOURITE MOVIE
Napoleon Dynamite. Yay!

FAVOURITE ACTOR
Denzel Washington

FAVOURITE ACTRESSES
Jessica Alba and Halle Berry

FAVOURITE SINGERS
Bob Marley, Beyoncé, Mariah Carey, Whitney Houston, Destiny's Child, Kanye West, Sean Paul and Jay-Z

> 'MY TOUGH CHILDHOOD MADE ME THE PERSON I AM TODAY.' R

PETS
Two dogs, DJ and Marley. Cute!

FAVOURITE DESSERT
Cheesecake or chocolate ice cream, and a bit of fruit if she's feeling healthy!

FAVOURITE CLUB IN BARBADOS
The Boatyard

ALTERNATIVE CAREER
If she hadn't been a singer, Rihanna would have loved to be a DJ

BEST FRIEND
Melissa (her assistant)

TATTOOS
Rihanna is a sucker for body art – she has fifteen tats (and counting!). Among them are a music note on her ankle, a star in her left ear, the word 'love' on her left middle finger, a trail of stars going down her back and the phrase 'shhh…' on her right index finger. She is crazy for them!

> 'I THINK WHAT MY FANS ENJOY ABOUT ME ARE MY FLAWS AND IMPERFECTIONS. THE FACT THAT I'M REBELLIOUS AND DO THINGS MY WAY MOTIVATES THEM TO BE INDIVIDUALS. THAT'S ALL I CARE ABOUT, YOU KNOW, PEOPLE BEING THEMSELVES AND LIVING LIFE TO THE FULLEST.' R

THE PATHWAY TO FAME!

A STAR IS BORN

On 20 February 1988, Robyn Rihanna Fenty was born on the beautiful Caribbean island of Barbados. Mum Monica, an accountant, and dad Ronald, a warehouse supervisor, were over the moon when they were handed their tiny baby daughter.

She was drawn to music from a young age and started singing when she was just three years old. Her dad heard her singing as she was lying on the bed using a hairbrush as a microphone and knew that their little girl was going to grow up to be super-talented. Then, when she was seven years old, her parents heard her singing the Disney classic 'A Whole New World' with their neighbours and they were amazed at how powerful her voice was.

Dancing shoes

But it wasn't just a talent for singing that Rihanna was blessed with – she loved to dance and she had a great sense of natural rhythm. But although you'd never guess it today, Rihanna was a shy child and never liked to take part in school productions, preferring to sing at home in the privacy of her own room. She spent hours after school playing with her childhood pal, Shakira. The pair were like sisters. Can you imagine?!

'WHEN I LEFT BARBADOS, I DIDN'T LOOK BACK. I WANTED TO DO WHAT I HAD TO DO TO SUCCEED, EVEN IF IT MEANT MOVING TO AMERICA.' R

Growing up

At home, Rihanna grew up with two younger brothers – and 13 male cousins! In fact, Rihanna and one of her cousins were the only girls amongst the family's kids, and Rihanna was a real tomboy! 'We had to fight to defend ourselves because the boys didn't want us around them,' she later remembered. 'We wanted to do what they did. We wanted to climb trees. We wanted to catch animals... We had to defend ourselves a lot!'

Despite all the tomboy activity, Rihanna was a good kid. She worked hard at school, and was respectful to her parents. But that doesn't mean she didn't have a good time and always made time for her mates and for having fun.

Rihanna's family always thought she'd go into business for herself. She was a very enterprising child – she used to sell things on the side of the road, selling hats and belts and scarves from a rack. She also bought sweets in bulk, put them in small packages and sold them onto her friends for a profit. The beginnings of an entrepreneur!

RIHANNA'S TOP TUNES

Everyone has a different Rihanna song as their favourite. Is it the catchy chorus for 'Umbrella', Rihanna's super-stylish look in 'What's My Name', or her duet with Eminem? Here are some of her no.1 hits

PON DE REPLAY
SOS
TAKE A BOW
RUDE BOY
LOVE THE WAY YOU LIE
UMBRELLA
WHAT'S MY NAME?

Rock fan

Did you know Rihanna is a big fan of rock music? As rihanna says, 'growing up in barbados, I wasn't exposed to a lot of rock music, we really love reggae and soca music and hip-hop. But when i moved to the united states last year, I was exposed to a lot of different types of music, rock being one of them, and I fell the song in love with it. [Now] I love rock music.' Her song 'kisses don't lie' from the girl like me album is a mash up of her two favourite genres – rock and reaggae!

Difficult times

But Rihanna's childhood was far from easy and her parents split up when she was fourteen. The experience has made Rihanna stronger and as she says 'I grew up fast, kind of like the second mum. My mum had to be a woman and a man, working for us all.'

Though she was very shy, she was as surprised as anyone when she won the school's beauty pageant talent show – winning, with her rendition of Mariah Carey's hit 'Hero' – not only did she beat girls two years older than her, she had found an outlet for her frustrations – through singing.

RIHANNA'S PARTY PLAYLIST

Rihanna knows a hit song when she hears one – but what does Rihanna listen to on her iPod? Here are some of her favourite tracks to kick back and party to!

1. 'Best I Ever Had'
   Drake

2. 'Closer'
   Kings of Leon

3. 'Young Forever'
   Jay-Z feat. Mr Hudson

4. 'Venus vs. Mars'
   Jay-Z

5. 'Meet Me Halfway'
   Black Eyed Peas

6. 'La La La'
   LMFAO

7. 'Throw It in the Bag (Remix)'
   Fabolous feat. Drake and The-Dream

8. 'Party in the U.S.A'
   Miley Cyrus

9. 'Thinking of You'
   Katy Perry

10. 'Umbrella'
    Rihanna feat. Jay-Z

11. 'Russian Roulette'
    Rihanna

12. 'Sweet Dreams'
    Beyoncé

13. 'Waiting on the World to Change'
    John Mayer

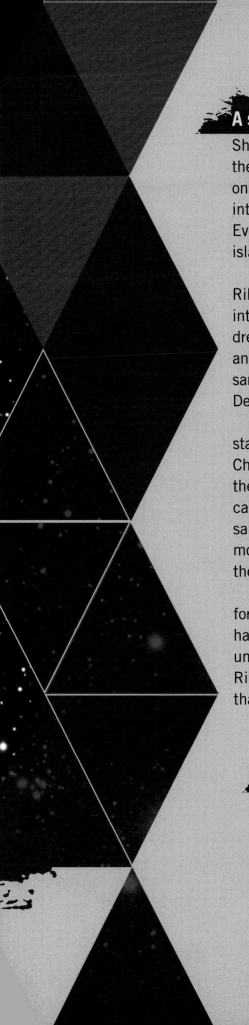

A step forward

She started a girl group with two of her classmates, and the three girls would practice together after school and on weekends. When Rihanna turned 15, some friends introduced the trio to the music writer and producer Evan Rogers, who was taking a holiday on the beautiful island of Barbados with his wife, Jackie.

An audition was arranged in Evan's hotel suite, and Rihanna and her friends – incredibly nervous – crept into the room, barely able to breathe. Rihanna was dressed in pink capri pants, a pink shirt and sneakers, and looked the completely angelic teenage girl. They sang 'Hero' by Mariah Carey and 'Emotions' by Destiny's Child.

Rihanna blew Evan – who had worked on hits for stars like Christina Aguilera, Kelly Clarkson and Christina Milian – away. 'The minute she walked into the room, it was like the other two girls didn't exist. She carried herself like a star even when she was 15,' Evan said later. 'But the killer was when she opened her mouth to sing "Emotion". She was a little rough around the edges, but she had this edge to her voice.'

He was so impressed with Rihanna that he asked for a second meeting with her and her mum. Rihanna had just come from school and was in her school uniform! After a serious chat with Monica, Evan invited Rihanna to New York to record a demo sometime over that coming year.

Call back

He understood that education was important, so agreed to fix the recording sessions in the school holidays. But he didn't count on how serious Rihanna was about pursuing her dream. She and mum Monica travelled back and forth between Barbados and Evan Rogers' home in Connecticut, where the young singer was given the benefit of Evan's vast experience and knowledge.

Sweet 16

Just after she turned 16, and following many long talks with her mum, Rihanna moved from her sunny home of Barbados to America, where she moved in with Evan and his wife to work on her music full time. They hired a tutor to help Rihanna finish her schooling (on strict instructions from her mum!).

Evan Rogers – along with his production partner, Carl Sturken – signed Rihanna to their production company Syndicated Rhythm Productions, and gave the 16-year-old her own lawyer and manager to ensure her best interests were taken care of.

Evan and Carl worked on demos tapes in the studio that were designed to show Rihanna's edgy side.

In January 2005, Evan and Carl finalised the four-song demo and sent it around to all the major labels in America, trying to drum up interest for their new client. Almost within hours, the hip hop label Def Jam responded, via a phone call from their newly appointed president, the rapper and producer, Jay-Z!

Big moves

When Jay-Z had heard the demo for 'Pon de Replay', he had been unsure about Rihanna, purely because he knew instantly the song would be such a hit. 'When a song is that big, it's hard for a new artist to come back from,' he said. 'I don't sign songs, I sign artists. Some people chase the hot song for a minute. I want to sign an artist based on the level of talent, the writing. I was a little reluctant.'

But he decided to make his decision after meeting the Bajan beauty. So RiRi was called to the Def Jam offices in New York to audition. She sat in the lobby waiting to be seen, shaking with nerves.

Star struck

'I was like: "Oh my, he's right there, I can't look, I can't look, I can't look!"' she said later. 'I remember being extremely quiet. I was very shy. I was cold the entire time. I had butterflies. I was so star-struck!'

Rihanna had never even met a celebrity before – and here she was, about to audition for one of the world's biggest stars! She was hysterical, but as soon as she stepped into the office she felt totally at ease. Jay-Z was welcoming and friendly, and Rihanna immediately felt at home there. She stood in the middle of the room and sang three songs for her small audience: Whitney Houston's 'For The Love of Me', 'Pon de Replay' and another song that had been written by Evan and Carl, called 'The Last Time'.

Her audition was a resounding success. 'From meeting her at 4pm in the office till 3am, I was absolutely certain,' Jay-Z said later. 'That doesn't happen too often!'

'THE AUDITION DEFINITELY WENT WELL – DEF JAM LOCKED ME INTO THE OFFICE - TILL 3AM! AND JAY-Z SAID, "THERE'S ONLY TWO WAYS OUT. OUT THE DOOR AFTER YOU SIGN THIS DEAL. OR THROUGH THIS WINDOW..." AND WE WERE ON THE 29TH FLOOR. VERY FLATTERING!' R

PICTURE
SUDOKU!

Fill in the boxes so each box contains a drawing of Rihanna with red hair, Rihanna with black hair, Katy Perry, Jay-Z, Beyoncé and Mariah Carey. Don't forget every row across and column down must contain all six pictures, so use a pencil before using a pen just in case you make a mistake.

TASTY TREAT TIME: BAJAN PUDDING!

She might be a picky eater, but when it comes to Bajan food, Rihanna loves it all – especially this recipe for Bajan Pudding! It might sound simple, but it's one of Rihanna's favourites – and one of ours, too!

YOU WILL NEED

400g plain flour

300g white sugar

400g butter

500 ml milk

4 eggs

1 teaspoon baking powder

1 teaspoon vanilla extract

1 teaspoon almond extract

What to do:

1. Preheat your oven to 205°C. Lightly grease and flour a 10-inch round cake pan.

2. Put the butter and sugar together in a bowl and cream them with a spatula until the mixture is light and fluffy. Add the eggs and beat the mixture well.

3. Sift the flour through a sieve and add that and the baking powder to the butter mixture, along with half the milk.

4. Make sure you carry on beating the mixture well. Add the remaining milk along with the vanilla and almond extracts. Pour batter into your pan.

5. Bake the pudding at 160°C for 1 hour (for a fan assisted oven). Reduce the heat to 140°C and continue baking for 15 minutes longer.

6. Eat – and enjoy!

MUSIC OF THE SUN

From signing to Def Jam, suddenly, Rihanna's work schedule went through the roof. They started prepping release of her debut album, *Music of the Sun*, which was released in August 2005. The album was a huge pop hit across the world – *Rolling Stone* described it as 'a seductive mix of big-voiced R&B and souped-up island riddims – what Beyoncé might have sounded like if she had grown up in the West Indies and skipped the whole Destiny's Child thing.' Wow!

'2005 TAUGHT ME THE DEDICATION AND RESPONSIBILITY IT TAKES TO MAKE THIS DREAM A REALITY … IT ALWAYS SEEMED GLAMOROUS – BUT IT IS REAL WORK. MY LOVE FOR MUSIC AND SINGING WILL NEVER CHANGE, BUT THE ROSE-COLOURED GLASSES ARE NO LONGER SO ROSY.'

Rockstar

Helped along by the smash single 'Pon de Replay' and a tour supporting pop icon Gwen Stefani, *Music of the Sun* peaked at number 10 in the American charts, and went on to sell over 2 million copies worldwide. Insane! Touring with Gwen also changed RiRi's view of other kinds of music. 'Coming from Barbados, I really hadn't heard that much rock music,' she said later. 'Touring with Gwen changed my perspective.' The experience would go on to influence the sound of her future albums!

A GIRL LIKE ME

Almost as soon as *Music of the Sun* had been released, RiRi was back in the studio, where songwriters and producers had already started to work on her second album. The album was called *A Girl Like Me*, and was scheduled to be released in April 2006 – just eight months after her debut hit the charts!

Knowing that Rihanna was a new artist and he had to work hard to establish her in the music scene, label boss Jay-Z set up a hectic work schedule for the teenager, making her work at breakneck pace. 'She was a new artist, and we were trying to get her to as many ears as possible,' he said later. *A Girl Like Me* was another chart smash, and it featured radio friendly singles 'SOS', 'Unfaithful' and 'Break It Off'.

A Girl Like Me smashed into the charts – going into the top 10 of 11 countries, spending a total of 415 weeks in pop charts and selling over two million copies worldwide. Wow!

Although her singles were doing really well in the charts, there was also the dark side of fame to battle against. The papers were full of false rumours about RiRi. At first the gossip made Rihanna laugh – but after a while, it started getting on her nerves. 'I just ignore it and I'm numb to it,' RiRi said wisely. 'You cannot stop people from saying what they want to say.'

'**A GIRL LIKE ME** IS A MORE PERSONAL ALBUM. I LOVE MUSIC OF THE SUN BUT THAT WAS MORE OF A PARTY ALBUM ... A FUN ALBUM. **A GIRL LIKE ME** IS FUN, GETS EMOTIONAL SOMETIMES (AND IS) JUST MIXED WITH A LOT OF DIFFERENT TYPES OF MUSIC, STYLES AND FLAVOURS.' R

GOOD GIRL GONE BAD

Rihanna had been working so hard – getting up at 5am every morning, doing interviews, live performances and constantly travelling – that label boss Jay-Z started worrying she might burn out. He ordered her to take a few months off to return to her home of Barbados for a well-earned vacation.

But after spending a few weeks back there – eating some home-cooked meals, tanning on the beach and catching up with her family and friends – RiRi was restless. She wanted to get back into the studio. 'I guess that has a lot to do with my youth. Younger people are usually very restless and can't keep quiet. But I am also very passionate about what I do!'.

Time out

So she returned to America earlier than planned, ready to work on her new album. But the time off at home had given her the chance to think, and the pop princess decided that she wanted to make some changes to 'Brand Rihanna'. She moved out of the home she had shared with Evan and Jackie Rogers, and moved into her own apartment in LA. She bought a huge grand piano and some bright pink artwork to decorate the pad in her distinctly Rihanna style.

Independence

She fired her original hair stylist and fashion stylist and hired new ones in an attempt to move away from her innocent girly image to a new, edgier style that represented her personality.

This new independence also sneaked into the studio. The sound of her first two albums had been largely influenced by her label, Def Jam, but for her third album, RiRi wanted to make a rebellious statement. She invited producers and songwriting talent like Justin Timberlake, Ne-Yo, Timbaland and Tricky Stewart into the studio to work with her, and the result was an edgy, rock-driven pop masterpiece.

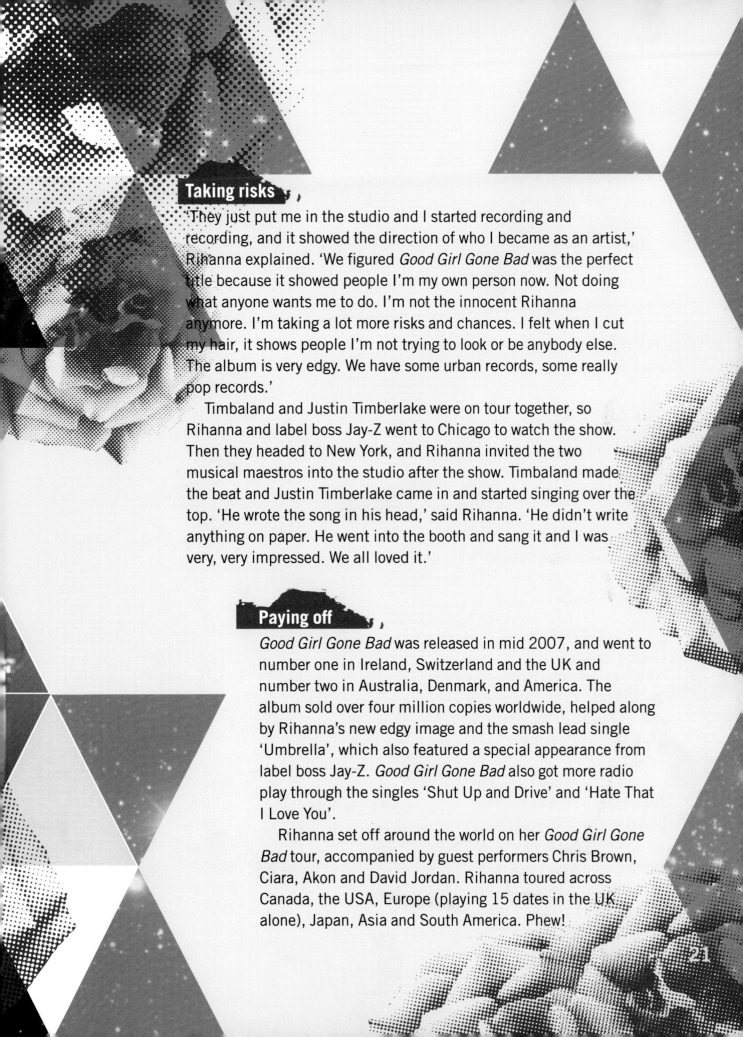

Taking risks

'They just put me in the studio and I started recording and recording, and it showed the direction of who I became as an artist,' Rihanna explained. 'We figured *Good Girl Gone Bad* was the perfect title because it showed people I'm my own person now. Not doing what anyone wants me to do. I'm not the innocent Rihanna anymore. I'm taking a lot more risks and chances. I felt when I cut my hair, it shows people I'm not trying to look or be anybody else. The album is very edgy. We have some urban records, some really pop records.'

Timbaland and Justin Timberlake were on tour together, so Rihanna and label boss Jay-Z went to Chicago to watch the show. Then they headed to New York, and Rihanna invited the two musical maestros into the studio after the show. Timbaland made the beat and Justin Timberlake came in and started singing over the top. 'He wrote the song in his head,' said Rihanna. 'He didn't write anything on paper. He went into the booth and sang it and I was very, very impressed. We all loved it.'

Paying off

Good Girl Gone Bad was released in mid 2007, and went to number one in Ireland, Switzerland and the UK and number two in Australia, Denmark, and America. The album sold over four million copies worldwide, helped along by Rihanna's new edgy image and the smash lead single 'Umbrella', which also featured a special appearance from label boss Jay-Z. *Good Girl Gone Bad* also got more radio play through the singles 'Shut Up and Drive' and 'Hate That I Love You'.

Rihanna set off around the world on her *Good Girl Gone Bad* tour, accompanied by guest performers Chris Brown, Ciara, Akon and David Jordan. Rihanna toured across Canada, the USA, Europe (playing 15 dates in the UK alone), Japan, Asia and South America. Phew!

BEST FRIENDS FOREVER

Katy Perry

Katy Perry and Rihanna couldn't be a better match made in heaven if they tried – the all-singing, all-dancing popstars were destined to be best friends. Not only are they two of the biggest popstars in the world, but they have the same fun-loving, bubbly personalities. 'We just clicked', says Rihanna. 'We have similar personalities and a similar sense of humor and from there she just seemed like a really down to earth person. In this industry you don't meet a lot of people that are genuine, but Katy is such a free spirit, she has no edit button!'

Their careers have also followed the same path. With catchy debut singles, both Rihanna and Katy shot into the charts at number one, and took the pop world by storm. Maybe it had something to do with their bold fashion sense and brightly coloured hair? Both Ri Ri and Katy aren't afraid to express themselves, and we love them for it! It's no wonder the girls have so much to talk about. With the release of their own perfumes, countless number one hits and some of the brightest hair in Hollywood, these girls are going to take over the music industry with their infectious songs and enviable style!

But they remember to keep their feet firmly on the ground. Rihanna was reportedly Katy's maid of honour in her marriage to Brit comedian Russell Brand, and even helped to plan her hen do! Although RiRi couldn't make the wedding, her pal didn't forget her. Rihanna's absence didn't upset Katy – in fact, if anyone knows a busy schedule, it's Mrs. Brand! The future looks bright for the BFFs, with a duet lined up next year. 'We want to get in the studio and hopefully make something for this album, who knows - or maybe for Katy's re-release', says Rihanna. 'We want to do something together for sure.'

The Texan beauty Beyonce got a taste for fame at a young age – just eight years old! She met her Destiny's Child bandmates (including her BFF Kelly Rowland!) on the audition circuit, and after her band-manager Dad retired to look after them, they were on their path towards fame. But it wasn't always a smooth ride for B and her friends. Their hard work finally paid off though – when Beyoncé was 15 that she and her bandmates got the big break they had been dreaming of, a record deal! A number one single soon followed in 'Jumpin' Jumpin'', which shot into the top of charts and stayed there for 14 weeks.

But at 21, Beyoncé decided to go it alone – and she never looked back! She's gone on to sell over 75 million records worldwide, with catchy anthems such as 'Single Ladies' and 'Crazy in Love' and has even sang for the US president! And when the multi-talented singer isn't on stage she is an award-winning actress, with starring roles in *Pink Panther*, *Austin Powers* in *Goldmember*, and *Dream Girls*. It's no wonder then that she is one of Rihanna's role models!

Jay-Z

Jay-Z is one busy man! Not only is the most successful hip-hop artist in the world and married to the 'Crazy in Love' singer, Beyoncé, but he is also a super-smart businessman! He runs his own clothing line, Rocawear, which celebs like Victoria Beckham and Madonna love to wear, wrote his own book, and founded his own record label, Roc Nation. It's no surprise then that the savvy entrepreneur became a mentor to the talented Rihanna!

Like Rihanna, Jay-Z has a very strong work ethic. Life wasn't also so glamorous for Jay-Z – the Brooklyn-born rapper had a very modest life as a child. His mum bought him a stereo after he kept his sibling awake at night playing the drums on the kitchen table – and the rest is history! Now a Grammy-award winning artist, Jay-Z has worked with the biggest stars in the world, including Kanye West, Ne-Yo and Coldplay. Is there no stopping him?

RATED R

For her next album *Rated R*, Rihanna reconnected with her label mate Ne-Yo, who worked with her on several tracks ('Stupid In Love' and 'Russian Roulette'). 'Rihanna is not in the same place mentally as she was before,' said Ne-Yo while they were recording the album. 'She's more comfortable in her skin now. She's just realised some things about herself that she can explain better than I can. I'll say this: It's refreshing to watch.'

Rihanna also called in some other production talent to help her craft the album, including StarGate, The-Dream, will.i.am, Brian Kennedy and British electronica duo Chase & Status. She also worked with upcoming singer and songwriter, Nicki Minaj. The album moved into darker musical territory, and had elements of hip hop, rock and dubstep alongside the usual pop sound that made her a global superstar.

RATED R PRODUCED FIVE HIT SINGLES ('Hard', 'Rockstar 101', 'Russian Roulette', 'Rude Boy', and 'Te Amo') and received good reviews from critics and RiRi's fans. The album reached the top ten position in ten countries (going to number one in Norway and Switzerland, and hitting number nine in the UK), and sold nearly three million copies worldwide.

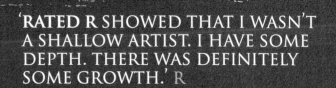

'**RATED R** SHOWED THAT I WASN'T A SHALLOW ARTIST. I HAVE SOME DEPTH. THERE WAS DEFINITELY SOME GROWTH.' R

Controversial choices

The single 'Russian Roulette' was one of the most controversial choices to include on the album. It was Rihanna's close relationship with Ne-Yo that allowed them to collaborate on the track. 'It just all came together – Rihanna has never been one to be afraid to take a chance, especially with me. She's always game to do something a little different. I played it for her, and she loved it – went in and knocked it out. The rest is history.'

Finding her focus

To promote the album, Rihanna hit the road for the *Last Girl On Earth* tour. 'I like to think about myself as 'The Last Girl on Earth' because sometimes people make decisions based on the outlook of others and, to me, my life is my life,' explained Rihanna. 'It's my world, and I'm going to live it the way I want to. That's how I think about everything, that way I'm focused on me, and my work. It's a really narrow space, a focus.'

The tour featured Pixie Lott, Tinchy Stryder, Tinie Tempah, Ke$ha and Calvin Harris among the support acts who wowed thousands of screaming fans across the world with Princess RiRi. Sensational!

SAY WHAT? QUIZ

How well do you know the girl called Robyn? Find out in our quiz!

**WHO PUTS IN A SPECIAL
GUEST APPEARANCE ON UMBRELLA
WITH RIHANNA?**

Ne-Yo

Jay-Z

Justin Timberlake

Timbaland

**HOW MANY VIEWS HAVE RIHANNA'S
VIDEOS HAD ON YOUTUBE?**

One billion

Ten million

Half a million

Fifty million

**WHAT TATTOO DID RIHANNA GET
ON HER 18TH BIRTHDAY?**

Poison ivy strand on her thigh

Pisces star sign symbol behind her ear

Pistol on her ankle

Champagne bottle on her wrist

WHAT IS RIHANNA'S FAVOURITE FOOD?

Fresh salad

Sushi

Steamed vegetables

Fried flying fish with cou-cou

**WHAT'S HER FAVOURITE PLACE
OUTSIDE OF BARBADOS?**

London

Sydney

Hawaii

Tokyo

**WHICH TRIO OF ARTISTS INSPIRED RIRI TO START
SINGING?**

Beyoncé, Mariah Carey, Whitney Houston

Soft Cell, Human League, Gary Numan

New Kids On The Block, Take That, Boyzone

The Supremes, Stevie Wonder, Michael Jackson

WHERE DID RIHANNA GROW UP?

Parish of St. Julian

Parish of St. Michael

Parish of St. Elvis

Parish of St. Stephen

**WHAT'S HER FAVOURITE WAY
OF KEEPING IN SHAPE?**

Hitting the gym

Going out jogging

Rehearsing and performing on stage

Aerobics classes

**HOW MANY SIBLINGS DOES
RIHANNA HAVE?**

Two – two sisters

Three – three sisters

Two – a brother and a sister

Two – two brothers

**WHO DOES RIHANNA LOOK UP TO
AND ADMIRE?**

Kate Moss

Barack Obama

Oprah Winfrey

Madonna

Answers on page 61

LOUD

2010 was to be a lucky year for the Bajan singer. In January she won her second Grammy for 'Run This Town'; a collaboration with Kanye West, who she had always wanted to work with, and her label boss, Jay-Z. In the summer of 2010, she collaborated with rapper Eminem on his number one hit 'Love The Way You Lie'. The track became Rihanna's seventh number one hit in America – a huge achievement for such a young talent!

In demand

Between the *Last Girl on Earth* Tour shows, interviews and fashion shoots, 22-year-old Rihanna also found the time to get back in the studio to work on her fifth album. Around 100 writers and producers were invited to different songwriting and production camps between studios in Los Angeles and Miami, where they wrote and put together songs for Rihanna and her management to consider. Among them were her old collaborators Stargate, The Runners, Polow da Don, Tricky Stewart, and Alex da Kid among others.

'We gave them guidelines and a bunch of topics,' Rihanna said later. 'We'd have 10 writers in one room and five writers in another room and put them with one producer, then split the group up and put them with another producer.'

Working hard

The whole process was fairly regimented, but RiRi had learned a strict work ethic from her mentors, and was keen to keep up the momentum. Never one to take a day off, when she bumped into Canadian rapper Drake backstage at an awards show, she played him 'What's My Name', and asked him if he'd perform on the song.

'Drake is the hottest rapper out right now and we've always been trying to work together,' she said. 'He's the only person I thought could really understand the melody of the song, and the minute he heard it he said, "I know exactly what I'm going to do. I love it." And he did it three days later.'

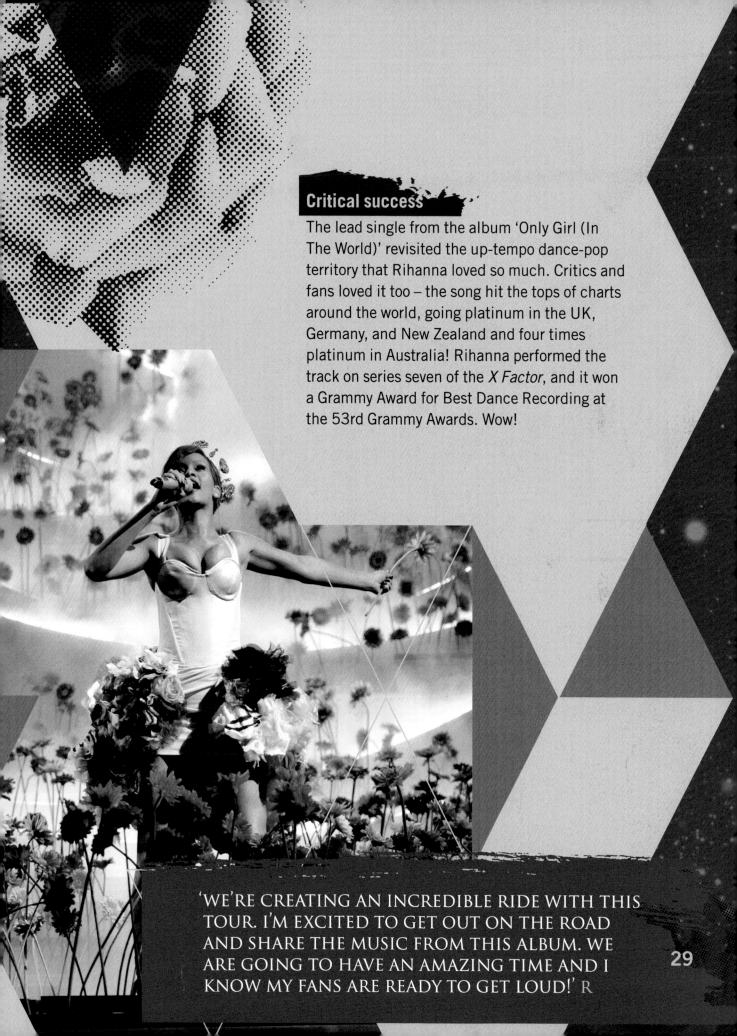

Critical success

The lead single from the album 'Only Girl (In The World)' revisited the up-tempo dance-pop territory that Rihanna loved so much. Critics and fans loved it too – the song hit the tops of charts around the world, going platinum in the UK, Germany, and New Zealand and four times platinum in Australia! Rihanna performed the track on series seven of the *X Factor*, and it won a Grammy Award for Best Dance Recording at the 53rd Grammy Awards. Wow!

'WE'RE CREATING AN INCREDIBLE RIDE WITH THIS TOUR. I'M EXCITED TO GET OUT ON THE ROAD AND SHARE THE MUSIC FROM THIS ALBUM. WE ARE GOING TO HAVE AN AMAZING TIME AND I KNOW MY FANS ARE READY TO GET LOUD!' R

Collaborating

Princess RiRi also had the chance to work with other top talent on *Loud*, including fellow female solo artist, Nicki Minaj. 'I couldn't wait to work with her and finally have her on my record,' said Rihanna. She loved the track they worked on together 'Raining Men'. 'It's a really fun song,' said Rihanna. 'Nothing like the original. It's quite uptempo but kind of quirky and funny. Nicki has a great buzz and she has a "thing" to her. She is a star and that's why people love her. She's also really entertaining with her visual as well as her lyrics, and she has a great melody.'

Twitter fans!

The album *Loud* was released in November 2010 and hit the top 10 in 16 different countries across the world. It sold over 300,000 copies in its first week alone, spurred on by the singles 'Only Girl (In the World)', 'What's My Name?' and 'S&M'. In March 2011, Rihanna asked her fans on Twitter what they thought the next single from Loud should be, and the fans told her – they wanted The Runner's track 'California King Bed'!

Promoting the album, RiRi planned a huge world tour – the *Loud* tour – that kicked off in America in April, running all the way through 2011 and taking RiRi into arenas across the world.

ON FACING THE HATERS

'I have been ready for the backstabbing my whole life. After I won the school talent show and beauty pageant. I lost a lot of people who i thought were my friends. But the people who are real have stuck around. When I signed my recording deal, a few fake friends and I parted ways. I gained some who wanted to get close to me because of the deal, so they had to go as well.' R

TRUST

'With success has come a lot of great stuff, but there are cons, too. Who to trust is a huge one. I always have to keep my guard up. A lot. I'm dealing with fake people. All the time. So i just keep my guard up.'

VITAL STATISTICS

Rihanna's smash single 'Umbrella' reached number one in 27 countries and sold over nine million copies worldwide, making it the best selling single in the world in 2007. The song won a grammy award, two billboard awards, and two mtv video music awards.

What does the Last Girl On Earth need?

Rihanna's backstage rider for her *Last Girl on Earth* tour was revealed in the gossip columns – and it was pretty far from what you might expect! RiRi requested a plush white six-foot couch (for her to take a nap on), white tulips, no harsh lighting, a 'thin' full-length mirror, icy blue chiffon to decorate the space, six throw pillows and a rug, all of which must be in cheetah or leopard print, and, most importantly, 'NO sequins' anywhere in RiRi's vicinity!

Getting her tweet on

2010 was the year that Rihanna started making a real connection with her fanbase. 'I just felt like there was this big distance with me and my fans,' she said. 'You know, they love me, they love how I dress and they move to my music, but they don't really know who I am.' So she decided to make a change, and in August 2010 she took over her Twitter account (which had only been used by her label up to then) and started directly communicating to her fanbase. Check her out @Rihanna!

RIHANNA QUIZ

1. **WHAT IS RIHANNA'S FULL NAME?**
A   Rochelle Fenty
B   Rihanna Robyn Fenty
C   Rayven Rihanna Fenty
D   Robyn Rihanna Fenty

2. **WHERE IS RIHANNA FROM?**
A   New York
B   Puertico Rico
C   Panama
D   Barbados

3. **WHAT WOULD RIHANNA HAVE BEEN IF SHE WASN'T A SINGER?**
A   DJ
B   Chef
C   Actress
D   Lawyer

4. **WHEN WAS RIHANNA BORN?**
A   May 29, 1987
B   July 15, 1989
C   October 13, 1988
D   February 20, 1988

5. **WHAT WAS THE NAME OF RIHANNA'S FIRST SINGLE?**
A   'Pon de Replay'
B   'Make Her Feel Good'
C   'Move Ya Body'
D   'Girlfight'

6. **WHAT WAS RIHANNA'S FIRST ALBUM CALLED?**
A   *Music of the Sun*
B   *Rihanna*
C   *Afrodisiac*
D   *Pon de Replay*

7. WHO WROTE RIHANNA'S 'UNFAITHFUL?'

A Jay-Z

B Pharrel Williams

C Diddy

D Ne-Yo

8. ON A GIRL LIKE ME'S FIRST WEEK OF RELEASE, HOW MANY COPIES WERE SOLD IN THE UNITED STATES?

A Over 200,000

B Over 150,000

C Over 125,000

D Over 115,000

9. WHICH SONG FROM *GOOD GIRL GONE BAD* WAS THE FIRST TO BE RELEASED AS A SINGLE?

A 'Umbrella'

B 'Pon de Replay'

C 'SOS'

D 'Don't Stop the Music'

10. IN WHICH MOVIE DID RIHANNA MAKE HER BIG SCREEN-ACTING DEBUT?

A *Beauty Shop 2*

B *Bring It On 3*

C *Mission Impossible 3*

D *Stick It*

11. WHICH GROUP'S MUSIC IS SAMPLED ON THE SONG 'SOS'?

A Culture Club

B Depeche Mode

C Naked Eyes

D Soft Cell

12. IN WHAT YEAR DID RIHANNA MOVE TO THE US?

A 2003

B 2004

C 2005

D 2006

13. WHICH RECORD LABEL IS RIHANNA SIGNED TO?

A Cash Money

B Def Jam

C LaFace

D Warner Bros.

14. NAME THE SLOW BALLAD THAT HAS CHANGED RIHANNA'S IMAGE AS A PERFORMER OF DANCE SONGS?

A 'We ride'

B 'SOS'

C 'Unfaithful'

D 'If it's loving that you want'

15. WHICH SPORTS BRAND HAS RIHANNA MODELLED FOR?

A Nike

B Adidas

C Reebok

D Puma

16. WHO WAS RIHANNA'S TOURING PARTNER FOR THE PROMOTION OF HER FIRST ALBUM, *MUSIC OF THE SUN?*

A Nelly Furtado

B Christina Aguilera

C Hilary Duff

D Gwen Stefani

17. WHO DID RIHANNA PLAN A WEDDING FOR?

A Beyoncé

B Alicia keys

C Her mum

D Katy Perry

18. WHICH WAS THE FIRST RIHANNA SINGLE TO TOP THE BILLBOARD CHARTS?

A 'Pon de Replay'

B 'SOS'

C 'If it's loving that you want'

D 'Unfaithful'

19. WHO WAS THE MUSIC PRODUCER WHO DISCOVERED RIHANNA'S TALENT WHEN HE WAS VACATIONING IN BARBADOS WITH HIS WIFE IN 2003?

A Phil Ramone

B John Pearson

C Christopher Walken

D Evan Rogers

20. WHAT WAS THE PEAK POSITION ATTAINED BY RIHANNA'S DEBUT SINGLE 'PON DE REPLAY' ON THE BILLBOARD TOP 100S CHART?

A 1

B 2

C 3

D 4

HOT STYLE SECRETS

It can't have escaped your notice that Rihanna is one of the hottest gals on the planet right now. With a style all her own, Princess RiRi has legs that are sky high and an attitude that's pure sass!

HUMBLE BEGINNINGS

Though she's always had striking looks, Rihanna was never much for indulging in makeovers or the like when she was younger. A self-confessed tomboy, she only started wearing makeup after she won the Miss Combermere Beauty Pageant at her school, when she was 15 years old. 'It was very new and weird to me,' she said. 'Only in high school did I start getting fussy with myself. That's when I started being very aware. But every woman has an ugly day!'

Girly girl

When Rihanna first moved to America, she relied heavily on advice about her style from her mentor Evan and her record label, Def Jam. She was dressed very much in casual island fashions, baggy pants, trainers, cropped tops and with her long wavy sunkissed tresses. Relying on the fashion and hair stylists that had been hired for her, RiRi started experimenting with top label designers like Dolce & Gabbana and Giuseppe Zanotti. But her style remained girly – her hair often pinned back into a bun, and wearing dresses and skirts that were a respectable length.

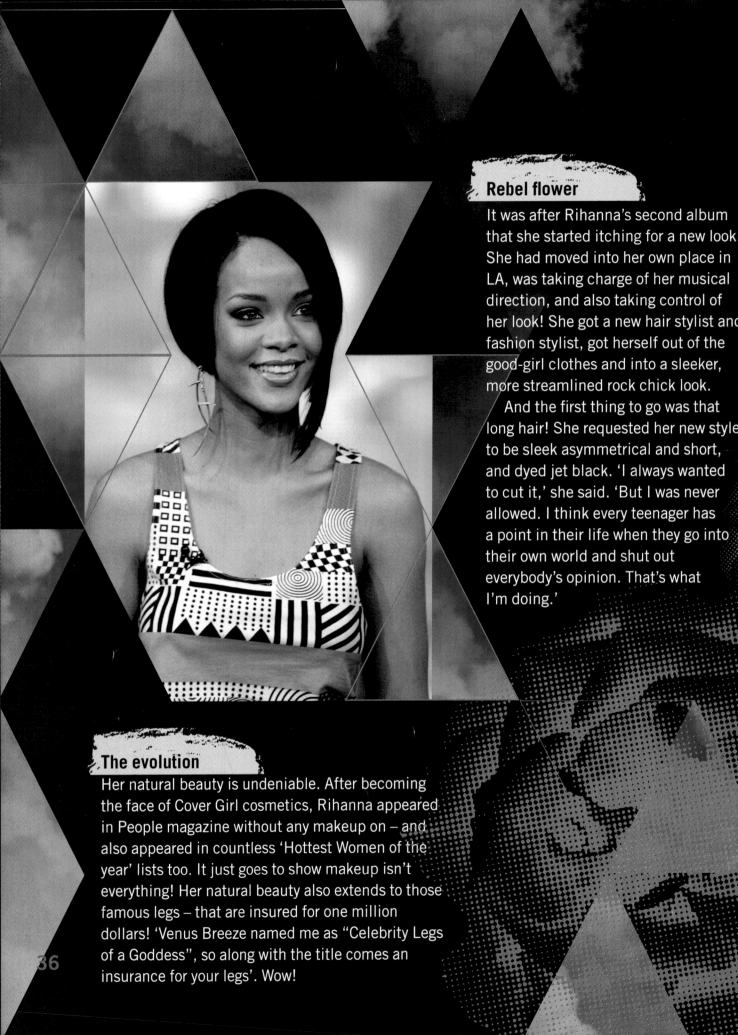

Rebel flower

It was after Rihanna's second album that she started itching for a new look. She had moved into her own place in LA, was taking charge of her musical direction, and also taking control of her look! She got a new hair stylist and fashion stylist, got herself out of the good-girl clothes and into a sleeker, more streamlined rock chick look.

And the first thing to go was that long hair! She requested her new style to be sleek asymmetrical and short, and dyed jet black. 'I always wanted to cut it,' she said. 'But I was never allowed. I think every teenager has a point in their life when they go into their own world and shut out everybody's opinion. That's what I'm doing.'

The evolution

Her natural beauty is undeniable. After becoming the face of Cover Girl cosmetics, Rihanna appeared in People magazine without any makeup on – and also appeared in countless 'Hottest Women of the year' lists too. It just goes to show makeup isn't everything! Her natural beauty also extends to those famous legs – that are insured for one million dollars! 'Venus Breeze named me as "Celebrity Legs of a Goddess", so along with the title comes an insurance for your legs'. Wow!

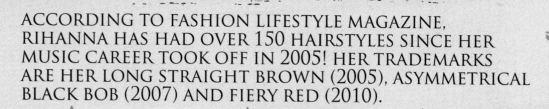

ACCORDING TO FASHION LIFESTYLE MAGAZINE, RIHANNA HAS HAD OVER 150 HAIRSTYLES SINCE HER MUSIC CAREER TOOK OFF IN 2005! HER TRADEMARKS ARE HER LONG STRAIGHT BROWN (2005), ASYMMETRICAL BLACK BOB (2007) AND FIERY RED (2010).

Dyed hair

'I wanted something that was a new look,' she said. 'Something, again, that wasn't the typical. Black hair is my favourite colour on me. I wanted something that was really expressive and vibrant.' Since then, Rihanna's style has changed more times than you could possibly keep track of. Her hair has been a shock of red, shaved on one or both sides, short and quiffed.

'It's really adventurous – I wanted something that was fun,' she says, about her constantly changing hair. 'I didn't want a normal hair colour. I'd had blonde and it was so boring. Black is still my favourite, but I was looking for a colour that was edgy … I couldn't do green or purple or pink, so red was like the fine line between normal and extreme!'

So how often does Rihanna go to the hairdresser? A lot! Her stylist goes to wherever RiRi might be, but she has to get my hair done often as there's a lot of maintenance needed with shorter hair. 'I have to get my sides cut all the time, and with the colour I've added another layer of difficulty. I have to pay close attention so I spend a lot of time with my hairdresser!' she says.

Fashion inspiration

You might not guess it, but Brit supermodel Kate Moss is one of RiRi's fashion icons. 'I see Kate Moss and just think about her style,' says RiRi. 'It's completely effortless with her and so true to who she is. It's always spontaneous, it's never thought out, or put together, it's just there and her hair is always messy. She doesn't care who is looking, or if there are paparazzi, and it works. She's a rock star!'

'THERE ARE DEFINITELY FEWER BLACK WOMEN IN THE HIGH-FASHION INDUSTRY. ONE OF THE THINGS I RESPECTED MOST ABOUT GUCCI WAS THAT THEY DID A PRINT CAMPAIGN WITH ME. I'M A BLACK GIRL ON A FASHION SPREAD FOR GUCCI – THAT WAS A BIG DEAL. I RESPECT DESIGNERS WHO AREN'T AFRAID TO GO OUTSIDE THE BOX. I WENT TO A JEAN PAUL GAULTIER SHOW, AND I SAW GIRLS WHO ARE BIGGER THAN ME, BEAUTIFUL AND VOLUPTUOUS AND DIFFERENT ETHNICITIES. THAT MADE ME SO EXCITED. I THOUGHT, OKAY, I CAN WORK THAT, FOR SURE.' R

'THE BEST THING ABOUT GOING WITHOUT MAKEUP IS THAT IT TAKES A LOT LESS TIME TO GET READY. YOU DON'T HAVE TO WORRY ABOUT MASCARA SPILLING OR EYELINER RUNNING OR ABOUT TOUCHING UP DURING THE DAY. YOU CAN WASH YOUR FACE AT ANYTIME. YOU FEEL COMFORTABLE AND FREE.' **R**

Body beautiful

'I have realised that I actually like my body, even if it's not perfect according to the book,' she says. 'For the first time, I don't want to get rid of the curves. My body is comfortable, and it's not unhealthy, so I'm going to rock with it!' Wise words for everyone!

'FASHION HAS BECOME MORE ABOUT TAKING A RISK. WHEN I AM PUTTING LOOKS TOGETHER, I DARE MYSELF TO MAKE SOMETHING WORK. I ALWAYS LOOK FOR THE MOST INTERESTING SILHOUETTE OR SOMETHING THAT'S A LITTLE OFF, BUT I HAVE TO FIGURE IT OUT. I HAVE TO MAKE IT ME. I THINK THAT'S THE THRILL IN FASHION.' **R**

'I LOVE ALEXANDER WANG, LOVE GIVENCHY, LOVE ALEXANDER MCQUEEN, HUSSEIN CHALAYAN, GAULTIER. SOMETIMES I WORK WITH THEM ON DESIGNING A CUSTOMISED LOOK FOR MYSELF WHICH IS ALWAYS FUN' **R**

GET THE RIHANNA LOOK!

One of RiRi's key makeup trends is her smoky eyes. That's a look she's been rocking since she hit the charts back in 2005! Follow the simple instructions below to recreate that sultry smoky look! Remember if you're going for smoky eyes, make sure to keep your lips nude – and if you're doing big lip make up, keep your eyes minimal, or you'll end up looking like a clown!

GET YOUR LIDS READY

The way that RiRi's makeup artist stops the eye shadow from falling away into the eyelid crease is to make sure her eyelids are oil free. This is done by first wiping the eyelids with primer, or base. Wipe this across your eyelid and make sure your eyelids are dry.

EYELINER

Now, apply your eyeliner. For a more conservative look, use a black, brown or grey liner to line above the upper lash line. Make sure you draw the line thicker from the middle of the eye outwards. For a wilder look, use blue, green or purple glitter liner.

Apply your liner to the bottom lid below the lashes, and then use your finger to smudge the line, getting that smoky look going.

EYESHADOW

Apply a nice cream shade for your base colour, and then whip a shimmery eyeshadow colour over the lids up to your eyebrow bone. Then add your darker eyeshadow colour to your lids, but make sure you keep the darker colour below the crease on your eyelid.

THE BLEND

Using a small eyeshadow brush, blend in the colour starting at your eyelash line and working upwards in small strokes. You need to blend the colour into your eyelash line so that your eyeliner disappears. Make sure your darker colour doesn't creep out – it needs to stop at the crease.

PERFECTION!

Check your artistic handiwork, correct any small errors or blend more with an earbud. Then to finish off, lashings of mascara, or perhaps some fake eyelashes if you're feeling in the mood!

DRESS LIKE RIHANNA

Rihanna has at all – not only does she have an amazing voice, a celebrity BFF and jet-set lifestyle, but she is one of the world's most famous style icons! But how does the superstar stay on top of the latest trends? She makes her own, that's how! Take a look at what makes Rihanna's look so unique and how you can shake up your own wardrobe, Rihanna style.

HAIR CARE

From an asymmetrical bob or fiery red curls, Rihanna isn't afraid to experiment with her hair colour or style. The style queen knows the quickest way to revamp your look it to change your locks! Why not try crimping, curling or pinning your hair? In true Rihanna style, try a different do for every day of the week…

SHADES OF GLAMOUR

Now she is one of the biggest stars on the planet, Rihanna is rarely seen out in public without her trademark shades. And the princess of pop likes her sunglasses to be huge! And never one to be a wallflower, she makes sure that they are as stylish as the rest of her look. To give your glasses a Rihanna sparkle, try bold bright colours, or stick-on jewels.

COMBO QUEEN

One of Rihanna's top style secrets is her ability to combine looks – who would have thought a leopard print top would look good with a neon skirt? Rihanna did! Try mixing colours, fabrics and styles together. Remember, fashion is about confidence, so strut with your new style!

43

DRESS TO IMPRESS

The self-confessed tomboy knows how to transform her look from casual to catwalk in one outfit – a dress! And Rihanna likes her dresses to be bold. Bright colours are a must, as are asymmetrical lines, and experimental material. Raid your dress up box for a true Rihanna look. Think glitter, lace and feathers!

SHOES, GLORIOUS SHOES!

Whether she is on the red carpet, out with her BFF Katy Perry or chilling in LA, Rihanna is always sure to be in top-to-toe glamour. Known for sky-high heels and platform boots, the superstar knows how to make her shoes stand out. For the Rihanna look, dare to clash colours – bright purple with red, or hot pink and green?

BLING!

Rihanna is the princess of pop – and she has the jewels to prove it. Rihanna loves the layered look – lots of long beaded necklaces, sparkling diamonds and colourful jewels together.

CROSSWORD

ACROSS

1. What was Rihanna's first ever single?

2. What nationality is Rihanna?

3. What is Rihanna's real first name?

4. Who did Rihanna first support on tour?

5. What is Rihanna's last name?

DOWN

6. Who's wedding did Rihanna organise?

7. Who wrote Rihanna's song 'Unfaithful'?

8. What label is Rihanna signed to?

9. What country was Rihanna born in?

10. What brand has Rihanna represented?

RIHANNA
WORD SEARCH

G	H	D	D	E	T	D	F	E	O	W	Z	D	D	W
U	M	B	R	E	L	L	A	S	U	R	X	Z	E	D
L	C	G	G	X	D	C	V	T	B	L	Y	H	I	W
W	W	E	E	U	R	I	E	L	R	N	L	S	R	O
Y	A	L	P	E	R	E	D	N	O	P	T	Y	I	B
D	P	O	E	V	U	K	R	L	O	U	O	S	H	A
U	J	B	T	T	W	T	M	B	R	B	P	O	A	E
O	B	H	U	H	K	C	D	B	E	J	E	S	N	K
L	E	H	Y	M	G	E	I	D	D	Q	W	E	N	A
N	J	C	I	Z	S	A	U	H	L	Q	T	J	A	T
Z	F	A	C	O	K	R	V	U	H	U	A	G	Z	U
D	A	B	E	N	O	G	L	R	I	G	D	O	O	G
J	A	Y	Z	Y	T	T	Y	Q	O	T	J	E	S	M
P	Q	J	W	O	R	Q	Z	V	E	M	W	G	G	P
M	M	I	G	G	G	V	I	M	N	O	W	E	Z	Z

DISTURBIA

GOOD GIRL GONE BAD

JAY-Z

LOUD

PON DE REPLAY

RIHANNA

RUDE BOY

SOS

TAKE A BOW

UMBRELLA

LOVE & ROMANCE

Through her early teens, Rihanna was so busy concentrating on her career, she barely had time to sleep, never mind for boys! But of course, like all teenage girls, she made sure she found time to date, but it was always her career that came first.

RIHANNA AND CHRIS BROWN

RiRi's most famous relationship was with R&B singer Chris Brown. She had long admired Chris as an artist, and wanted to work with him early in her career. They were introduced by a mutual friend and worked together in the studio.

At first she refused to comment on their relationship, saying only that they were very good friends. But it didn't take long for the couple to be papped holding hands and getting very close on holiday together. But it wasn't long before Rihanna realised Chris wasn't the man for her – and moved on.

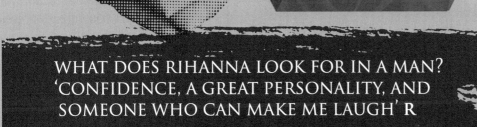

> WHAT DOES RIHANNA LOOK FOR IN A MAN?
> 'CONFIDENCE, A GREAT PERSONALITY, AND
> SOMEONE WHO CAN MAKE ME LAUGH' **R**

TODAY

Since her relationship with Chris Brown, Rihanna has stayed mostly single, although she has been on a few dates! She dated Los Angeles Dodgers' outfielder Matt Kemp for a while, and the couple seemed to enjoy each other's company. 'I have such a chaotic life, but at the end of the day, he is just my peace,' she said about her easy relationship with him. 'It keeps me sane, really, talking to him and talking to my family.'

But it wasn't to last. Rihanna was so busy with her music that she just couldn't find time to squeeze a man in as well. She's too involved with her work but for the time being, she's just happy being single. So what is she looking for in her soulmate? 'My favourite thing in a guy is his height. He has to be 6ft at least. He also has to know what he wants in life.'

LOOKING AT THE STARS

RIHANNA'S ASTROLOGY: PISCES

Rihanna has her star sign tattooed behind her ear so we know she takes her astrology seriously – but what does it mean? Rihanna's star sign is a pisces, which means she imaginative, sensitive, compassionate and kind. Sounds like the Rihanna we know! Her sympathetic side means that she understands people and their problems, meaning that she's always there lending a listening ear to her friends when they need her. Rihanna is an honest and super-patient friend – she sounds like the perfect BFF!

But on the other side, she can be quite vague and doesn't always want to make the decisions. Sometimes she can be led too much by her friends and doesn't always make the decisions that suit her the best. But we feel she's strong enough to stand up for herself!

At work, Pisces are best off working by themselves so it suits Rihanna being a solo artist rather than in a pop group or collaboration.

RIHANNA LIKES

HER PERSONAL SPACE
MYSTERY IN ALL ITS GUISES
SILLINESS – AS LONG AS IT'S FUNNY!

RIHANNA DISLIKES
THE OBVIOUS
BEING CRITICIZED
FEELING CONFUSED
KNOW-IT-ALLS

RIHANNA'S 2012 OUTLOOK

Rihanna's luck

Rihanna's luck lies in using the power of her personality to attract new opportunities. 2012 will feel like a real fresh start for Rihanna and she'll be feeling super confident going into the new year. It's time for her to let go off the past and cut off any loose ends.

Career and Finances

The year will start on a rather slow note, but everything will pick up in March when her assertive nature takes the lead. She may even pick up an award or too!

Love Life and Family

The later half of 2012 is set to be filled with friendship and love for Rihanna, with July – September being filled with romance, however RiRi needs to take care as there is a tendency to fall for people with complicated situations.

RIHANNA IS MOST
COMPATIBLE WITH
TAURUS
SCORPIO
CANCER
CAPRICORN

RIHANNA IS LEAST
COMPATIBLE WITH
ARIES
GEMINI
LEO
LIBRA
SAGITTARIUS
AQUARIUS

OTHER FAMOUS PISCES
INCLUDE:
EINSTEIN
DREW BARRYMORE
BRUCE WILLIS
HOLLY HUNTER

AND WHAT ABOUT YOU?

So we know who RIhanna is best suited to, but what about you? Take a look at the chart below to see who is your perfect cosmic match!

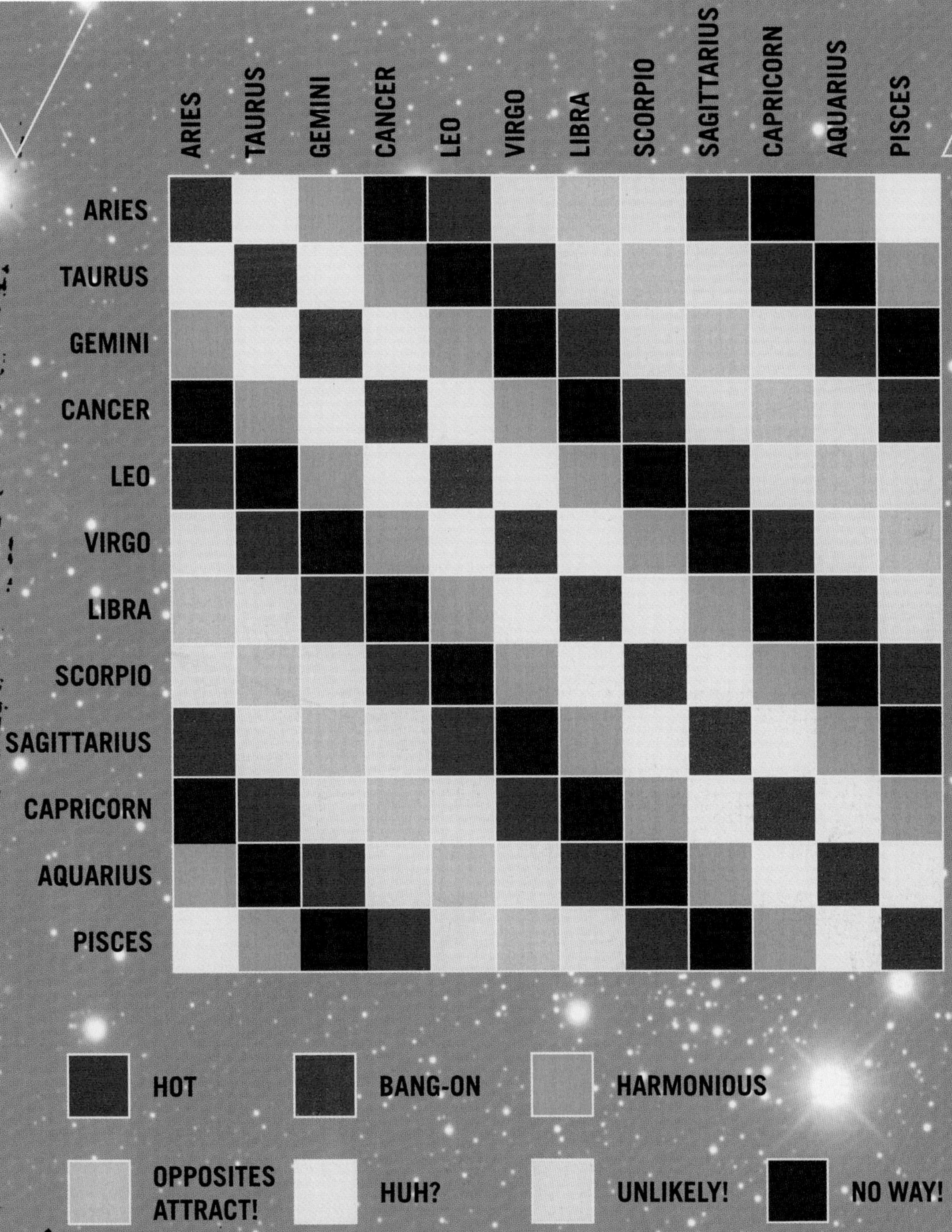
ARIES
TAURUS
GEMINI
CANCER
LEO
VIRGO
LIBRA
SCORPIO
SAGITTARIUS
CAPRICORN
AQUARIUS
PISCES
HOT
BANG-ON
HARMONIOUS
OPPOSITES ATTRACT!
HUH?
UNLIKELY!
NO WAY!

RIHANNA QUICK FACTS!

Rihanna is one of the talked our about popstars in the world, but test your friends and find out if they knew these top facts!

WHEN SHE WAS YOUNGER, RIHANNA'S MOTHER WAS A PROFESSIONAL MAKE UP ARTIST BUT WOULDN'T ALLOW HER DAUGHTER TO USE BEAUTY PRODUCTS. RIHANNA GREW UP AND BECAME THE FACE FOR COVER GIRL COSMETICS.

AT THE 2007 AMERICAN MUSIC AWARDS, RIHANNA WON THE FAVOURITE FEMALE ARTIST FOR SOUL/R&B CATEGORY.

RIHANNA IS VERY PICKY WHEN IT COMES TO FOOD. SHE WON'T EAT MEXICAN, CHINESE, JAPANESE, OR INDIAN FOOD. SHE ALSO HATES VEGETABLES.

IF RIHANNA DIDN'T HAVE A MUSIC CAREER, SHE WOULD HAVE TO HAVE BEEN A DJ.

RIHANNA'S BIGGEST PET PEEVE IS WHEN PEOPLE ARE DISHONEST.

RIHANNA'S FAVOURITE SINGERS ARE BEYONCE, ALICIA KEYS AND WHITNEY HOUSTON.

IN FEBRUARY 2008, BARBADOS CREATED A NATIONAL HOLIDAY TO HONOUR RIHANNA. SHE ACCEPTED THE HONOUR AND AS A THANK YOU SHE PUT ON A FREE CONCERT FOR HER FANS. SWEET!

IN THE 2007 TEEN CHOICE AWARDS, RIHANNA WON IN THE CATEGORY CHOICE MUSIC: R&B ARTIST.

RIHANNA IS OF AFRICAN, CREOLE AND GUYANESE DESCENT.

RIHANNA IS THE OFFICIAL SPONSOR FOR THE BARBADOS TOURISM AGENCY.

RIHANNA IS TUTORED FOR 15 HOURS A WEEK.

DESIGN YOUR OWN RIHANNA T-SHIRT!

You've got tickets to her show – but what are you going to wear?? Show that you're the number one Rihanna fan by customising a t-shirt to prove your dedication. Display your awesome designs on the t-shirt panels, below!

THE FUTURE!

For a girl still in her early twenties, Robyn Rihanna Fenty has achieved a great deal in her life so far! Five hit albums, countless hit singles, cover shoots, endorsement deals … what else could there be for this feisty Bajan singer still to achieve?

'I ALWAYS WANTED TO MAKE A DIFFERENCE IN THE WORLD. I WAS ALWAYS TRYING TO FIGURE OUT HOW COULD I CHANGE THE WORLD. WHAT COULD I DO? I THINK THE AMERICAN WAY IS A FANTASY. PEOPLE LIVE WITH AIR IN THEIR HEAD, REALLY. THEIR PRIORITIES IN LIFE ARE FANCY CARS AND BLING. IN BARBADOS IT'S ALL ABOUT HAVING FUN, DEFINITELY, BUT ALSO ABOUT HAVING GOOD GRADES.' R

AS FOR WHAT LIES AHEAD, RIHANNA IS FULL OF PLANS – THINGS SHE WANTS TO ACHIEVE BEFORE THE GRAND OLD AGE OF 30! 'I want to venture off as an entrepreneur and have my own fashion and makeup lines – just experiment with the things that I love. I'm a rebel. A rebel flower,' she says. 'And that's girly, but tough too – there's always that strength and vulnerability. There's always something beautiful. But there's still an edge.' R

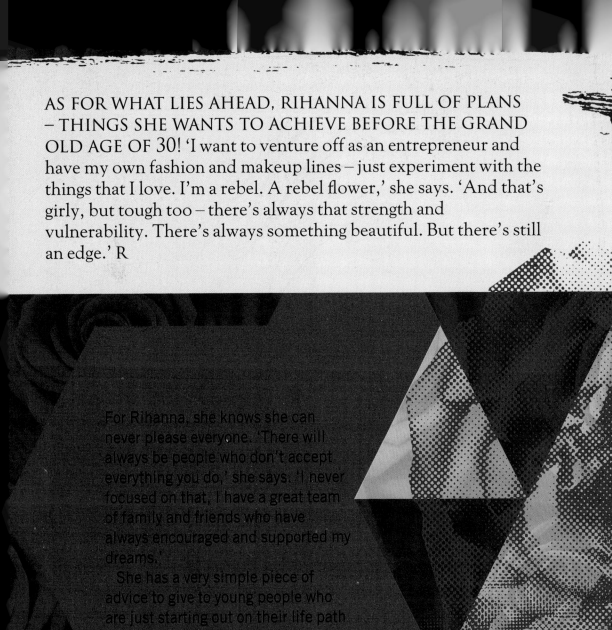

For Rihanna, she knows she can never please everyone. 'There will always be people who don't accept everything you do,' she says. 'I never focused on that, I have a great team of family and friends who have always encouraged and supported my dreams.'

She has a very simple piece of advice to give to young people who are just starting out on their life path and trying to succeed like her. 'Never give up on your dreams!' says Rihanna. 'Keep working, stay positive!'

AND WITH THE MOVIE **STARSHIP** IN THE WORKS FOR 2012 – AND A WHOLE GALAXY OF TOUR DATES TO GET THROUGH BEFORE THEN – WE'RE SURE THAT RIHANNA IS GOING TO BE RULING OUR WORLD FOR SOME TIME TO COME. GO RIRI!